Robert Ballard

by Bob Italia

Published by Abdo & Daughters, 6535 Cecilia Circle, Bloomington, Minnesota 55435

Library bound edition distributed by Rockbottom Books, Pentagon Tower, P.O. Box 36036, Minneapolis, Minnesota 55435

Library of Congress Number: 90-082623   ISBN: 0-939179-95-4

Cover Photo by : Bettmann Newsphotos
Inside Photos by: Bettmann Newsphotos and Woodshole Oceanography Institute

Edited by Rosemary Wallner

— Contents —

A New Breed of Explorer 5
Where Is the *Titanic*? 7
Exploring the Wreck 14
Where Is the Stern? 18
Ballard Returns to the *Titanic* 22
Inspecting the Gash 29
Farewell, Titanic 30

Dr. Robert Ballard holding a model of the Titanic.

A New Breed of Explorer

Of all the modern-day explorers, none can compare with Dr. Robert Ballard. He uses fantastic high-technology equipment to explore the ocean depths.

Ballard was born in Kansas in 1942, but spent most of his boyhood in California where he became interested in the ocean—particularly, what was beneath it. When he was a teenager, he took up scuba diving instead of surfing. Later, he studied geology and chemistry at the University of California, then went on to graduate school at the University of Hawaii and the University of Southern California where he studied oceanography. Ballard worked for Army and Navy Intelligence, then got his Ph.D. in marine geology and geophysics at the University of Rhode Island.

Ballard is one of the world's leading marine geologists. He is the senior scientist at Woods Hole Oceanographic Institute in Woods Hole, Massachusetts. At Woods Hole, scientists study the oceans of the world.

Ballard has developed underwater exploration technology including the *Argo/Jason* submersibles. These underwater diving machines allow scientists to explore the darkest depths of the world's oceans.

Ballard has made over fifty deep-sea expeditions using these high-technology vehicles. In 1977, he explored the bottom of the Pacific Ocean. There, he discovered hot air vents and huge tube worms. Ballard often writes about his underwater adventures in the *National Geographic* magazine.

But by far his most famous adventure occurred in the summers of 1985 and 1986. That is when Ballard and his expedition team used the *Argo* and *Jason* submersibles to explore a most famous shipwreck.

Ballard descended two-and-a-half miles to the ocean floor to explore the wreck of the *Titanic*.

Where is the Titanic?

How could it have happened? How could the unsinkable *Titanic* sink? Where exactly on the ocean floor was the *Titanic*? Was the ship still intact? These were some of the questions Dr. Robert Ballard pondered when he began his quest to find the *Titanic*.

Finding the *Titanic* seemed simple enough. It was a huge ship. Scientists knew the approximate area where the ship had sunk. Still, three expeditions had failed to find any traces of the once-mighty ship.

Ballard's quest for the *Titanic* had two parts. The first part involved the French ship *Le Suroit*. The crew on this ship would use sonar to locate the wreck. Then the crew on the American ship *Knorr* would use the submersible *Argo* to inspect the wreck and take photographs.

Just after midnight on April 15, 1912,
the grand ocean liner, Titanic hit an iceburg
and sunk into the icy waters of the Atlantic ocean.

Ballard joined the crew of the *Le Suroit* in July 1985. For three weeks, the crew searched for the *Titanic*. The ship's sonar unit, known as SAR, was sent to depths of 12,500 feet. The *Le Suroit* slowly dragged the unit over the ocean floor. SAR inspected the two-and-a-half mile area where Ballard thought the *Titanic* rested. As Ballard wrote, "the process was a bit like towing a kite on a two-and-a-half mile string."

They found nothing.

Did the *Titanic* fall into a massive underwater canyon? Or was it covered with mud, never to be found? These were the questions that haunted Ballard and his team as they were repeatedly frustrated over their lack of success.

By August 6, Ballard realized that the SAR unit would not be able to find the *Titanic*. The team needed more than just sonar. They needed to see what was on the bottom of the ocean. Ballard decided to bring in the American ship *Knorr* and its submersible *Argo*. The *Argo*, with its cameras, could find debris from the *Titanic* that the SAR could not locate. Ballard believed this would be the key to finding the *Titanic*.

Once the *Knorr* arrived in the search area, the *Argo* was launched. The *Argo* is an unmanned submarine with three television cameras. It is operated by remote control from the ship. The *Argo* immediately began searching the same two-and-a-half square mile area that the SAR had covered.

August 25: The *Argo*'s cameras showed nothing but mud and darkness.

August 26: The cameras picked up an underwater canyon, but still no debris.

Where was the *Titanic*? Ballard wondered.

On August 27, Ballard decided to expand the search area. He moved the search team southeast of where the *Titanic*'s lifeboats had been picked up seventy-three years earlier. These were unknown waters, far from the actual point where the *Titanic* had sunk. But Ballard had a hunch that the *Titanic*, during its long plunge to the ocean floor, had drifted southeastward just as its lifeboats had. It was just a hunch, but he decided to follow it.

More frustration followed the next few days as *Argo* failed to spot anything significant.

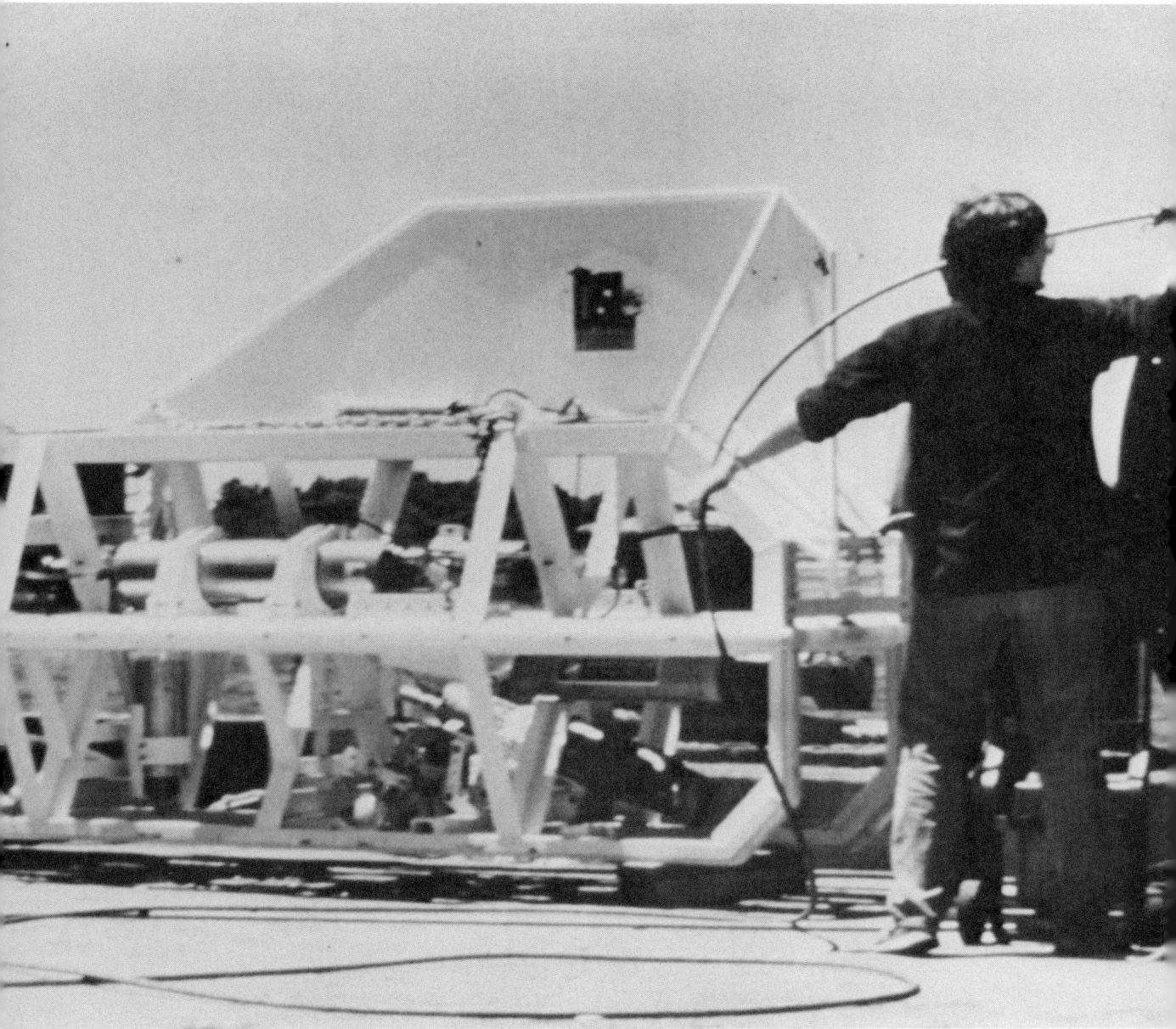

The Argo.

But on September 1, 1985, during what Ballard called the graveyard shift (the shift past midnight), the crewman operating *Argo* in the *Knorr*'s control room thought he saw something in the mud.

All *eyes were* glued to the television screen in the control room. The screen showed what *Argo*'s cameras were seeing.

Then came the exclamation: "Wreckage!"

Something man-made appeared on the screen, something circular.

"It's a boiler!" a crewman shouted.

It was part of the debris Ballard had been searching for. Somewhere nearby lay the huge wreck of the *Titanic*.

Ballard and his crew broke into joyous celebration. But then Ballard realized the true significance of his find, and his mood grew somber. It was nearly 2 A.M. now—the same hour in which the *Titanic* had sunk. Ballard stopped the expedition momentarily and went out on the deck of the *Knorr*. The others joined him. "I really don't have much to say," he said, "but I thought we might just observe a few moments of silence."

The memorial in honor of the *Titanic*'s victims lasted ten minutes, then Ballard said, "Thank you all. Now, let's get back to work."

An icebucket from the Titanic.

Exploring the Wreck

Ballard wanted to get as many pictures of the *Titanic* as he could. He wanted to show the world what the *Titanic* looked like after seventy-three years on the ocean floor. Was the ship in one piece? Was there anything left to explore? And what about the people who had died on the ship? Would there be any evidence of them?

Ballard had *Argo* photograph the debris field (the area where wreckage was found). *Argo* photographed a bent ship crane, twisted hull plating, and a crushed boiler. Despite the debris, Ballard was confident the ship was in one piece.

At this time, Ballard did not want to look inside the main wreck. If he was not careful, *Argo* could get caught in the wreckage. If it did, the expedition would be over. No one could go down and free the *Argo*. The water pressure at two-and-a-half miles deep was too great for humans, and would crush them.

Ballard decided to move the *Argo* over the main deck of the *Titanic*. But he was cautious. He would take *Argo* high over the deck, avoiding any possibility of collision or entanglement with the wreck.

Ballard brought *Argo* 164 feet above the ocean floor. Despite *Argo*'s bright lights, the crew could not see the mud bottom or the debris field anymore. They only saw dark ocean water. To locate the main wreck, Ballard turned on *Argo*'s sonar.

Immediately, the sonar told Ballard there was a massive object directly below.

Everyone in the control room was silent as they kept their eyes glued to the television screen.

"Down five meters," said Ballard to the crewman at *Argo*'s controls.

Argo slowly descended towards the main wreck.

Suddenly, Ballard saw something on the television screen. "It's the side of the ship," he said. "She's upright!"

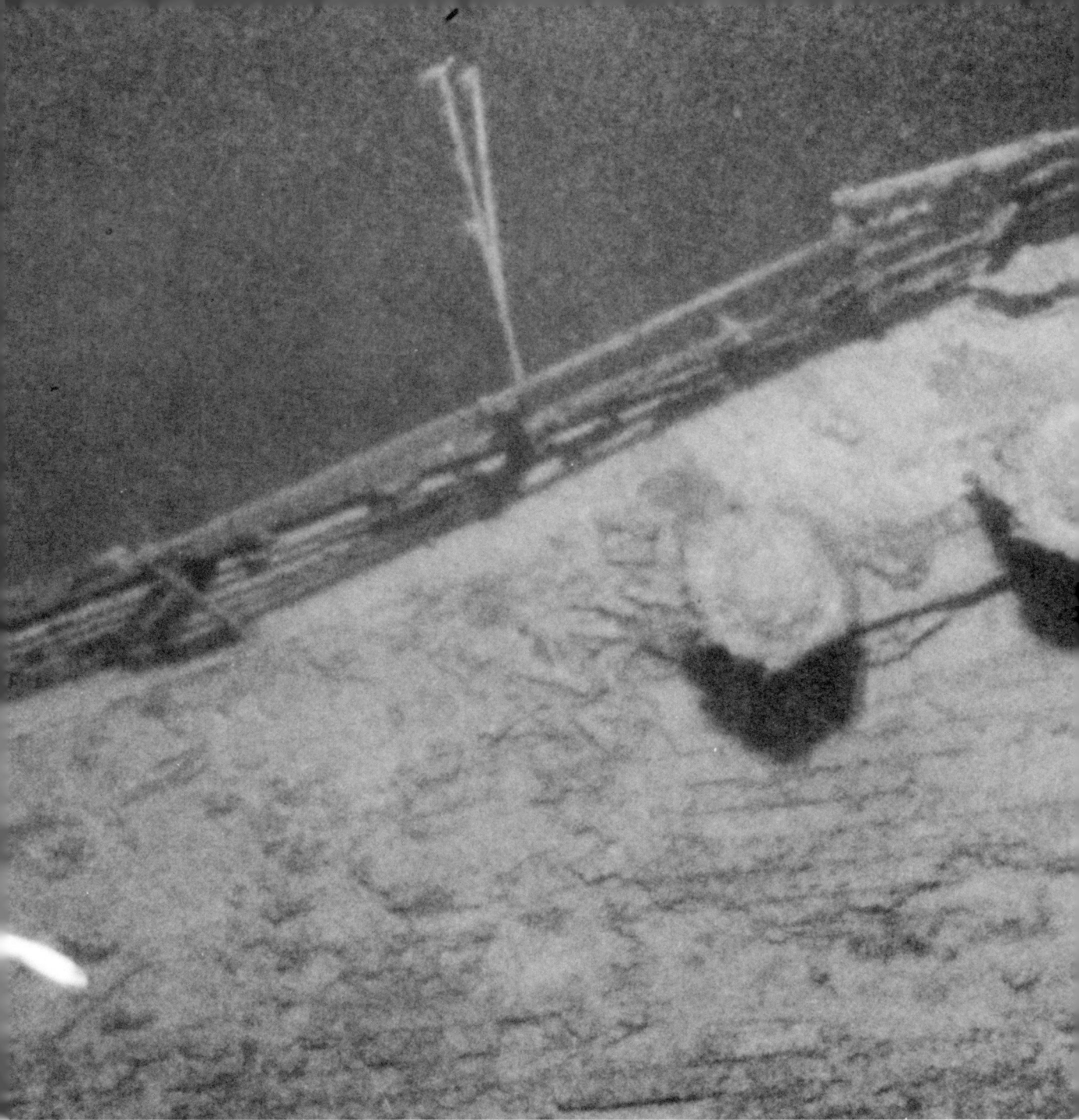

Part of the Titanic.

Now the *Titanic* was in view. Ballard and his crew were the first to see the famous ship in more than seventy years. When the *Titanic* went down, no one thought it would be possible for anyone to see the ship again. And yet, here they were, staring at the ship's deck.

The crew broke into spontaneous celebration. Ballard was numbed by his accomplishments. This was, by far, his greatest feat ever.

Argo spent six minutes viewing the main wreck. It appeared that the *Titanic* was in one piece. This was important. It would make the exploration much easier. Ballard would be able to easily identify specific locations on the ship.

Another pass was made over the *Titanic*, then another.

Suddenly, Ballard realized something was wrong.

Each time *Argo* swept towards the stern (rear) of the ship, the image of the *Titanic* turned into a mess of twisted steel, torn metal, and rubble. Ballard knew what this meant.

The entire stern section of the *Titanic* was gone. The *Titanic* had broken in two.

A storm on the surface of the Atlantic was brewing. Fearing that the rough seas would make it impossible to control *Argo*, Ballard brought *Argo* back to the surface. The hunt for the stern would have to wait.

Where is the Stern?

The storm raged for many hours. Ballard grew impatient and ordered the launching of the *Angus*. *Angus* is a submersible similar to *Argo*. But instead of television cameras, *Angus* has regular cameras that take still photographs.

Angus was sent down to take photos of the debris field. It photographed a hairbrush, bed springs, tea cups, dinner plates, and wine bottles.

Then Ballard ordered the *Angus* to photograph the main wreck. The *Titanic* expedition was just about over, and Ballard wanted photographs of the *Titanic* to bring back with him.

18

Angus.

Hours later, the *Angus* was pulled up from the wreck. It was time to return to the United States and show the world what had been discovered.

As they left, Ballard was not worried about losing the *Titanic*'s location. His crew had made careful maps of the area. It would be easy to locate the wreck when they returned.

Mobs of people greeted Ballard and his team at Woods Hole, Massachusetts. Ballard described the position of the ship to the crowd:

"The *Titanic* lies in 13,000 feet of water on a gently sloping alpine-like countryside overlooking a small canyon below. Its bow faces north and the ship sits upright on the bottom. There is no light at this great depth and little life can be found. It is a quiet and peaceful and fitting place for the remains of this greatest of sea tragedies to rest. May it forever remain that way and may God bless these found souls."

But where was the stern? Were there any bodies near the wreck?

These and many other questions would be answered later, during Ballard's return trip to the *Titanic* in 1986.

20

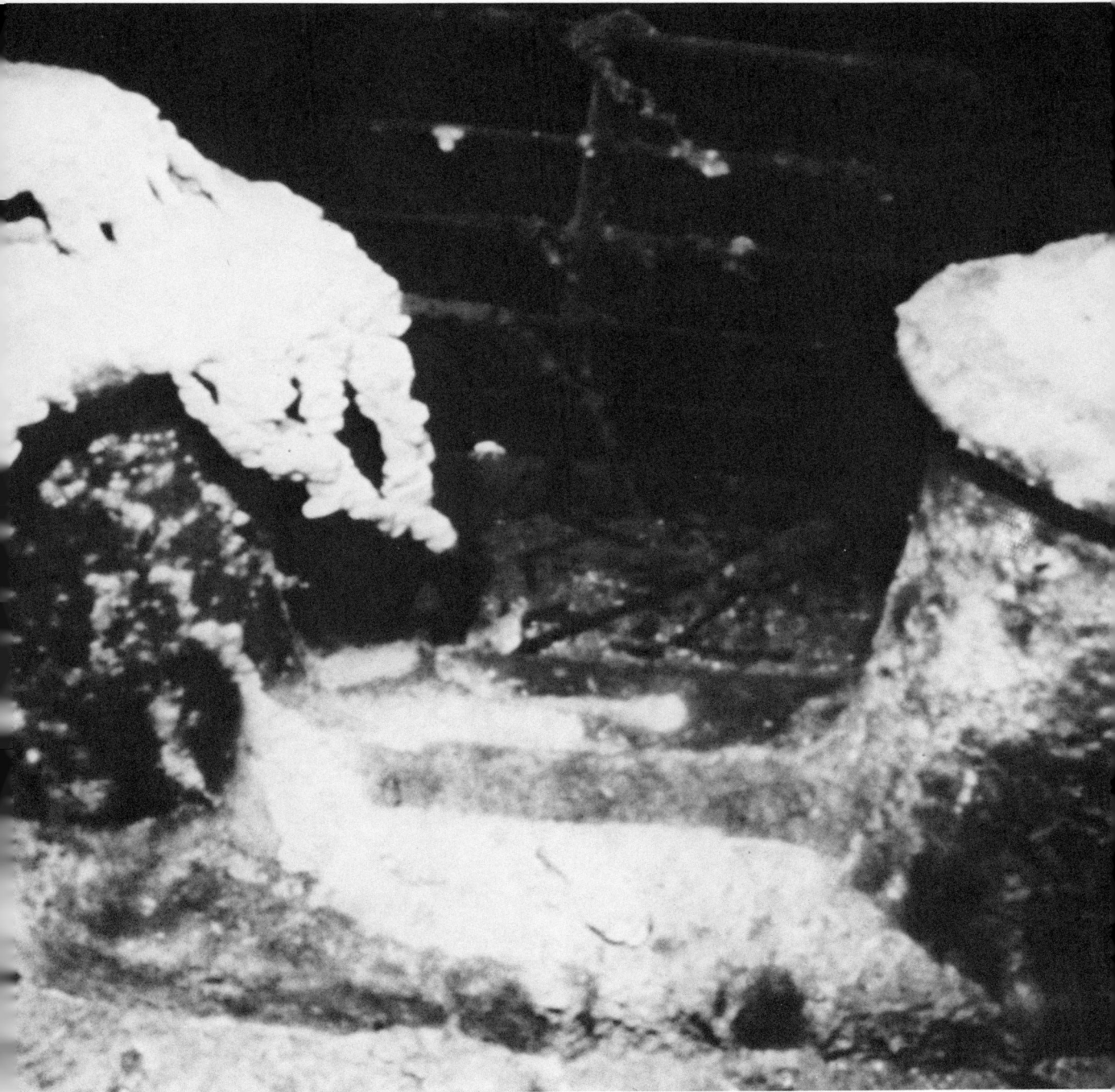

The submerged Titanic.

Ballard Returns to the *Titanic*

The second exploration of the *Titanic* began on July 12, 1986. This time, Ballard and his crew were aboard the *Atlantis* II. With them were *Alvin* and *Jason*.

Alvin is a small deep-sea submarine that can hold a three-man crew. During this exploration, Ballard would use *Alvin* to travel to the ocean floor and see the *Titanic* with his own eyes.

Jason would accompany *Alvin*. *Jason* is a small, remote controlled robot designed for underwater exploration. *Jason* would take photographs and would be small enough to go into the *Titanic*. *Alvin*, like *Argo*, was too big to enter the wreck.

Once their ship reached the *Titanic*'s location, Ballard and two crew members crawled into *Alvin*'s small interior. They switched on the controls and guided the craft down towards the wreck. The deep-sea ride lasted for over an hour and a half. It got very cold inside *Alvin*; outside it was very dark.

Finally, *Alvin* and her small crew reached the bottom. But Ballard still could not see any signs of the *Titanic*.

Alvin moved slowly across the bottom. It traveled to the spot where Ballard knew the *Titanic* rested. Suddenly, the seafloor began to slope upward, as if something huge had plowed it upward.

Ballard was excited. He knew the *Titanic* was just outside his submarine. "I think I see a wall of black just on the other side of that mud mountain," he told his crew.

This was it. The towering black hull of the *Titanic* loomed over the mud floor of the ocean.

Ballard was never so excited. Seeing the *Titanic* on a television screen was one thing. But seeing it with his own eyes, and actually being with the *Titanic* two-and-a-half miles below the surface of the ocean, was something only he and his two-man crew could experience.

Technical problems forced the crew to take *Alvin* back to the surface. But Ballard returned to the *Titanic* the very next day.

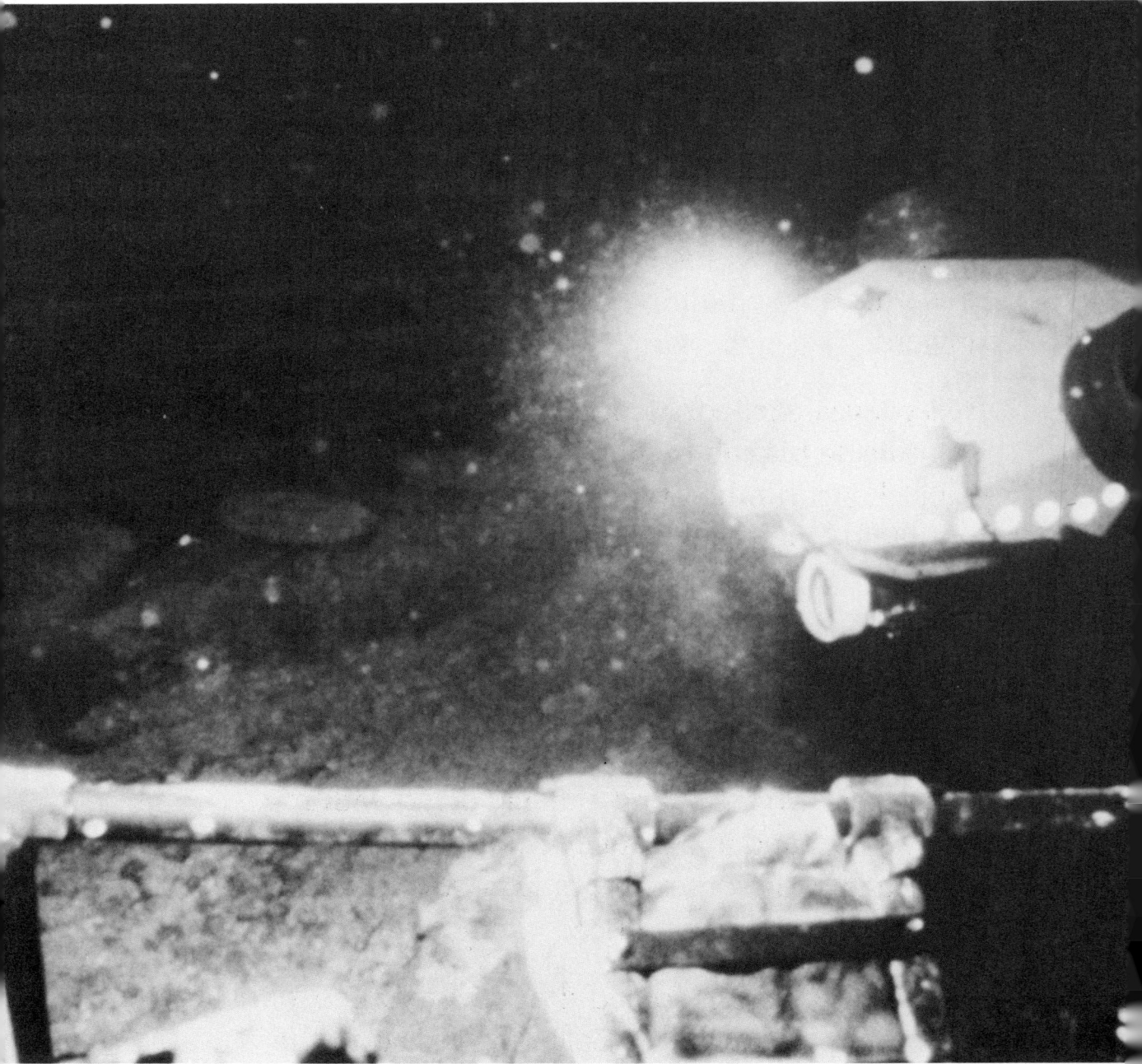

Alvin.

This time, Ballard landed *Alvin* at the pointy edge of the *Titanic*'s bow (front). He saw that the *Titanic* had buried its nose into more than sixty feet of mud. This had happened when the mighty ship crashed into the ocean floor.

The ship seemed to be oozing something. Streams of rust covered the hull. Decades of sitting in the saltwater had taken a heavy toll on the once proud ship.

Ballard directed *Alvin* upward over the deck of the ship. But there was no place to land. The wooden deck was gone. It had been eaten away by wood-boring mollusks. Undoubtedly, there would be little left to discover inside the ship. Anything made of cloth or wood also would have been eaten by the mollusks.

Ballard settled *Alvin* on one of the *Titanic*'s metal decks. They landed next to a gaping hole where the wooden grand staircase had once been. Next, Ballard launched *Jason* and directed it into the gaping hole. Soon the small robot was out of sight.

Ballard turned his attention to the video screen in *Alvin* that allowed him to see what *Jason* was viewing. He saw a big, dark room with what appeared to be pillars and a chandelier.

Ballard could not believe his eyes. Something as delicate as a chandelier had survived the violent two-and-a-half mile plunge to the bottom of the sea. Inside this room, some woodwork remained. Perhaps the mollusks had not destroyed all of the interior after all.

Alvin's batteries were getting low, so Ballard had to halt the day's journey. He directed *Jason* back to *Alvin* and radioed the crew on the *Atlantis II*.

The very next day, Ballard, *Alvin*, and *Jason* returned to the deep. They saw the wheelhouse, or what was left of it. Only brass fittings remained. All the wood was gone.

Ballard saw the ship's foremast (front mast). It had fallen backwards, its crow's nest still attached. He saw empty lifeboat davits (cranes) from which the lifeboats had been launched. And he saw the insides of the first-class staterooms. No wood, furniture, or bodies remained.

In the days ahead, More dives followed. The stern had not yet been located. But Ballard was moving slowly towards that direction.

During one dive, Ballard took *Alvin* to the debris field behind the main wreck of the bow section. There he found bottles, shoes, headboards, bathtubs, and sinks.

And then, Ballard came upon a safe.

Many wealthy people had been aboard the *Titanic*. They would have put their valuables in a safe until the voyage was over. Ballard could not resist using one of *Alvin*'s robot arms to latch onto the safe's handle to try to open it.

The arm grasped the handle, but the door was rusted shut. It refused to open.

Ballard tried to think of another way to open the safe, but gave up, wondering what kind of treasures lay inside. Later, while looking at photographs of the safe, Ballard realized the safe's bottom had rusted away. Nothing was inside the safe after all.

Another dive to the debris field was made. After much searching, Ballard located the stern section. It had landed 1,970 feet away from the bow section. The entire stern section had turned completely around.

Finding the stern solved one mystery. Some survivors had claimed that the *Titanic* had broken in two before it plunged to the bottom of the ocean. That now appeared to be true. Had the ship broken in two upon impact on the ocean floor, the stern would have been much closer to the bow section.

The stern was buried deep in mud. No propellers could be seen. They were buried, also. The stern was in much worse condition than the bow. Most of the stern's decks had collapsed upon themselves, making internal exploration almost impossible.

Before Ballard left the stern, he used *Alvin*'s robot arm to place a plaque on the hull of the ship. The plaque was in memory of those who had died on the *Titanic*.

Many more dives were made. *Alvin* and *Jason* made systematic journeys over the *Titanic*'s three main areas: the bow, the debris field, and the stern. Now Ballard had a map of the entire wreck. But there was one giant mystery that remained to be solved.

Why did the *Titanic* sink?

Inspecting the Gash

Everyone knew the *Titanic*'s collision with the giant iceberg had ripped a gash into the ship's starboard side. But was it the sole cause of the disaster? Or did something else happen to the ship that allowed the icy water of the Atlantic to flood the ship and cause it to sink? This is what Ballard wanted to find out.

On July 22, Ballard and *Alvin* photographed the entire starboard side of the bow. They looked for evidence of the huge gash. But because the point of the bow had buried itself deep in the mud, much of the supposed gash was also buried.

Ballard did see enough to draw this startling conclusion: the gash was not as great as everyone had thought, and probably not the single cause of the disaster. So why did the *Titanic* sink? Ballard cannot say for sure, only that the original claim of a huge gash probably is not true. Something else happened to the starboard side of the ship during the collision with the iceberg—something in addition to the gash. What exactly happened will probably never be known.

Farewell, *Titanic*

Ballard made his final dive to the *Titanic* on July 24, 1986. The money he got from the Navy to fund the expedition was running out, and the stormy season on the North Atlantic was approaching. After taking as many photographs of the *Titanic* as he could, Ballard laid one last plaque on the bow. Then he said good-bye to the mighty ship.

Ballard described his last moments with the *Titanic* this way:

"The sub (*Alvin*) paused for a moment, as if reluctant to leave the *Titanic* for the last time. Then we began to drift upward, accelerating toward the surface. I watched the video screen as the boat deck of the ship faded into the gloom; the last things I saw were the squashed roof of the officers' quarters and that lonely lifeboat davit..."

And so ended one of the most fantastic explorations man has *ever* attempted.

There has been talk by other deep water explorers of salvaging parts of the *Titanic*. But Ballard is fighting this proposed idea. He wants the *Titanic* to remain an honored gravesite. The United States Congress passed a law declaring the wreckage site an international memorial. Ballard hopes this will discourage anyone from bringing up *Titanic*'s artifacts.

But what is next for Dr. Robert Ballard and his technological wonders? The oceans of the world are littered with countless wrecks, many of them surrounded by mystery. Ballard has proven that man can explore just about anywhere—if he uses his imagination and intelligence.

Ballard will not say what great challenge he will tackle next. But when he makes his next dive, you can be sure the entire world will want to read all about it.